SÃO PAULO

THE CITY AT A GLANCE

Avenida São Luís

The slow revival of the downtown dis
breathing life back into what, in its
was São Paulo's equivalent of Fifth Av

Edifício Itália

One of the tallest buildings in South A
has impressive views across the city. H
to the 41st-floor Terraço bar for a suns
See p064

Edifício Copan

Oscar Niemeyer's building once housed
transvestite prostitutes. As the area improves,
so do the prices of its 1,160 apartments.
See p012

Ibirapuera Park

This is Niemeyer and Roberto Burle Marx's
modernist challenge to Central Park. Come
for the galleries and architecture, and stay to
see Paulistanos enjoying the great outdoors.
See p074

Former Hilton Hotel

When it opened in 1971, the Hilton was Brazil's
first luxury hotel. Its last guest checked out in
2004, but the circular tower remains a splendid
part of the cityscape, and is now home to the
Tribunal de Justiça do Estado (State Court).
Avenida Ipiranga 165

Museu de Arte de São Paulo (MASP)

Lina Bo Bardi's giant red box stands out among
the skyscrapers on Avenida Paulista. Inside is
South America's best collection of European art.
See p066

Jardins

The low-rise, high-priced districts of Jardim
Paulista, Jardim America and Jardim Europa
offer the city's best shops, eateries and hotels.

INTRODUCTION
THE CHANGING FACE OF THE URBAN SCENE

São Paulo is at last shaking off its undeserved image as a *Blade Runner*-esque sprawl of urban alienation. Its sheer size was often a factor that put off the casual visitor, yet South America's largest city has by nature always had more than its fair share of charms – if you knew where to look – as well as a unique energy, sophistication and modernist élan. And with Brazil's emergence as a global power, *Sampa* is currently on fire. The megacity is the gateway to a lucrative Brazilian market of 200 million people, and driven by the country's rapidly expanding middle class, São Paulo has become an economic powerhouse. An impressive group of homegrown designers and an effortlessly stylish population have turned it into a world-class shopping destination, and increasingly, an important centre for South American fashion and design. Meanwhile, its superb cuisine, nightlife and cultural diversions have always been a major draw.

It can be hard to avoid the frequent echoes of New York, thanks to the skyscrapers, the incredible immigrant mix, the eye-popping disparities in wealth and the rollerskating loons in Ibirapuera Park, which, designed by Oscar Niemeyer and Roberto Burle Marx, was meant to be an improvement on Central Park. And yet in São Paulo, you find a city so untrammelled by the tourist hordes that the locals turn out to be immensely friendly. Indeed, even the coolest and most beautiful can seem quaintly touched that a foreigner has had the *colhões* to visit their city. This can only change, so go soon.

ESSENTIAL INFO
FACTS, FIGURES AND USEFUL ADDRESSES

TOURIST OFFICE
Convention & Visitors Bureau
Alameda Ribeirão Preto 130
T 3736 0600
www.visitesaopaulo.com

TRANSPORT
Metro
T 3371 7411
www.metro.sp.gov.br
Trains run from 4.40am to midnight
(Sunday to Friday) and 1am on Saturdays
Helicopter
Brazilian Helicopter Services
T 21 2189 0050
www.bhs-helicopteros.com.br
Taxis
Rádio Taxi
T 3146 4000
It's advisable to call for a cab late at night

EMERGENCY SERVICES
Ambulance
T 192
Fire
T 193
Police
T 190
24-hour pharmacy
Drogaria São Paulo
Praça Julio Mesquita 131
T 3331 5273

CONSULATES
British Consulate-General
Rua Ferreira de Araújo 741
T 3094 2700
ukinbrazil.fco.gov.uk/en
US Consulate
Rua Henri Dunant 500
T 5186 7000
saopaulo.usconsulate.gov

POSTAL SERVICES
Post office
Rua Haddock Lobo 566
T 3083 2879
Shipping
DHL
Rua Bela Cintra 1165
T 3062 2152

BOOKS
Paulo Mendes da Rocha: Fifty Years
by Paulo Mendes da Rocha (Rizzoli)
**When Brazil Was Modern: A Guide
to Architecture 1928-1960** by Lauro
Cavalcanti (Princeton Architectural Press)

WEBSITES
Architecture
www.vitruvius.com.br
Newspaper
www.folha.com.br

EVENTS
Bienal
www.fbsp.org.br
Boom SP Design
www.boomspdesign.com.br
International Film Festival
www.mostra.org

COST OF LIVING
**Taxi from Guarulhos Airport
to Jardins**
R$105
Cappuccino
R$4
Packet of cigarettes
R$6
Daily newspaper
R$2.50
Bottle of champagne
R$210

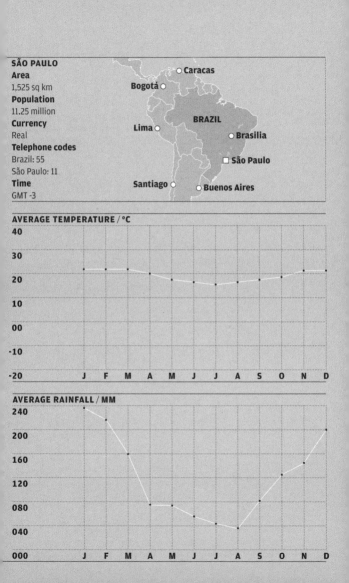

SÃO PAULO
Area
1,525 sq km
Population
11.25 million
Currency
Real
Telephone codes
Brazil: 55
São Paulo: 11
Time
GMT -3

Caracas
Bogotá
BRAZIL
Lima
Brasilia
São Paulo
Santiago
Buenos Aires

AVERAGE TEMPERATURE / °C

	J	F	M	A	M	J	J	A	S	O	N	D

AVERAGE RAINFALL / MM

	J	F	M	A	M	J	J	A	S	O	N	D

NEIGHBOURHOODS

THE AREAS YOU NEED TO KNOW AND WHY

To help you navigate the city, we've chosen the most interesting districts (see below and the map inside the back cover) and colour-coded our featured venues, according to their location; those venues that are outside these areas are not coloured.

JARDINS

The canyon that is Avenida Paulista marks the southern edge of downtown São Paulo, and beyond are the chic Jardim Paulista, Jardim América, Jardim Europa and the newly hip Baixo Jardins — which form a low-rise hollow of expensive homes and upmarket shopping, including NK Store (see p062) and Forum (see p084). Jardim Paulista is great for designer fashion and simply gazing at the beautiful people.

CENTRO

Not a place to wander at night, downtown São Paulo is nonetheless bustling by day. It may be more down-at-heel than the Jardins, but it has a big-city energy that makes so many compare São Paulo with New York. It also has a dizzying stretch of modernist landmarks near Praça da República, in the form of the Edifício Itália (Avenida Ipiranga 344), Oscar Niemeyer's Edifício Copan (see p012) and the former Hilton Hotel (Avenida Ipiranga 165).

VILA MADALENA

This creative neighbourhood is full of arty venues, small bars, restaurants and one-off stores — typical is Casa Palomino (790 Rua Mourato Coelho, T 3813 0414), which houses a gallery and bar, hosts events and publishes a fashion magazine. Look out for antiques and vintage clothing along Rua Fidalga, and take in an exhibition at the innovative Galeria Fortes Vilaça (Rua Fradique Coutinho 1500, T 3032 7066).

ITAIM BIBI

At the southern end of São Paulo's Wall Street, Avenida Brigadeiro Faria Lima, this mixed commercial and residential district has become an élite night-time hangout focused on Rua Amauri and Rua Dr Mário Ferraz. Stand-out venues include the Cuban-themed club Azúcar (Rua Doutor Mário Ferraz 423, T 3074 3737), lunch spot Forneria San Paolo (see p042) and restaurant KAÁ (see p045).

HIGIENÓPOLIS

Literally 'city of hygiene', Higienópolis was built above the festering downtown at the end of the 19th century to provide a haven for the rich. It's not São Paulo's hippest address, but the area is home to a fine collection of architecturally distinguished apartment blocks — Vilanova Artigas' Edifício Louveira (see p076), João Artacho Jurado's Edifício Bretagne (see p068), and Edifício Prudência (Avenida Higienópolis) by Rino Levi and Cerqueira César.

PINHEIROS CENTRO

This mixed *bairro* is a major socialising hub. It is home to Jun Sakamoto (see p040), one of the city's best Japanese restaurants, Mediterranean eaterie Chou (Rua Mateus Grou 345, T 3083 6998), with its charming garden, and Consulado Mineiro (Praça Benedito Calixto 74, T 3088 6055), a great place to sample the national dish, *feijoada* (black bean and pork stew), traditionally eaten on Saturday afternoons.

LANDMARKS
THE SHAPE OF THE CITY SKYLINE

Running the numbers on São Paulo is scary: more than 11 million people live in the city itself, and in the greater São Paulo area a total of 20 million souls are crowded together; some geographers insist on adding adjacent metropolises, such as Baixada Santista, São José dos Campos, Campinas and Sorocaba, to create what's called the Extended Metropolitan Area (Complexo Metropolitano Estendido), with nearly 28 million inhabitants. As populous cities go, that's a global second only to Tokyo, and it's a good six million more than the whole of Australia. These lucky folk live in a place three times the size of Paris – and growing – so it's easy to feel daunted, even a bit terrified, by the city. That is, until you decide to ignore the vast majority that has little to offer the visitor.

Your focus should be on downtown, known as Centro, and its immediate neighbours: the 'Little Tokyo' of Liberdade – if only for the food – and the original designer suburb of Higienópolis. The rest of the city worth exploring extends south-west through the affluent districts of Jardins, Vila Madalena, Pinheiros Centro, Itaim Bibi and around Ibirapuera Park (see p074). These are the areas that boast the shops, restaurants and architecture that make São Paulo such a rewarding destination if you're prepared to put in the legwork. Get your hotel to hook you up with a driver and you'll find there's little to be scared of – except, perhaps, the traffic jams. *For full addresses, see Resources.*

Memorial América Latina

Set in a vast plaza, this is Oscar Niemeyer's most criticised project – it was deemed austere and incoherent, and costing 10 times its budget didn't do it any favours. Opened in 1989, there are eight buildings serving political, cultural and leisure functions. Must-sees include the Pavilhão da Criatividade, with work by artist Tomie Ohtake and a collection of folk art; the cathedral-like Salão de Atos Tiradentes reception hall (above), the Victor Civita Library, home to 30,000 titles, as well as music and images; and the Símon Bolívar Auditorium, which hosts classical and opera performances. Access is via an elevated footbridge that offers a bird's eye view of the site or through a tunnel decorated with a mural by Sergio Ferro. *Avenida Áuro Soares de Moura Andrade 664, T 3823 4600, www.memorial.sp.gov.br*

Edifício Copan
Planned as a complex of shops, a hotel,
cinema and terraces, Oscar Niemeyer's
Copan ended up as 1,160 mixed-income
apartments with big curves and design
flaws – one of the characters in Regina
Rheda's *Stories From the Copan Building*
says: 'It's good for taking pictures, but lousy
to live in.' The ground-floor Bar da Dona
Onça (T 3257 2016) does a great *feijoada*.
Avenida Ipiranga 200

Pinacoteca do Estado

The State Art Gallery is a superb example of exactly how to get a cultural renovation right. The original building, the Liceo de Artes y Oficios (São Paulo Art School) was designed in Italian neoclassical style by Ramos de Azevedo in the late 19th century. Pritzker winner Paulo Mendes da Rocha did little to alter the exterior in his 1993 refurbishment, but replaced the roof with latticework glass atria to create covered courtyards and removed many interior walls to provide exhibition spaces, which are connected by elevated walkways. The Pinacoteca reopened in 1998 and, in 2000, da Rocha claimed a prestigious Mies van der Rohe Award for his design. The collection itself focuses on Brazilian art from the past two centuries.

Praça da Luz 2, T 3324 1000,
www.pinacoteca.org.br

HOTELS

WHERE TO STAY AND WHICH ROOMS TO BOOK

São Paulo has not traditionally been a tourist destination and, as recently as 2002, its tired hotel market reflected this all too well. The executive floor of the Renaissance (Alameda Santos 2233, T 3069 2233) was as good as it got, although, having said that, the view from the ridge on which the tower sits is one of the best in the city. The Maksoud Plaza (see p025) had always offered something a little different, if rather dated, but then came local architect Arthur Casas' Emiliano (see p026), the city's first upscale designer destination, which was quickly followed by the Fasano family's move from the restaurant business into the luxury hotel market (opposite). Architect Ruy Ohtake's outlandish Hotel Unique (see p029), known locally for obvious reasons as the Watermelon, has since joined them and exudes a sense of drama and technological brashness you will either love or hate.

The big chains have also upped their game. The Hilton (see p028) moved from downtown to Morumbi, while the Grand Hyatt (see p020) also provides corporate fare in the same area, which is convenient for the financial district around Avenida Faria Lima as opposed to Avenida Paulista or downtown. More affordable upscale accommodation is offered by the Normandie Design Hotel (Avenida Ipiranga 1187, T 3311 9855) and Pergamon (Rua Frei Caneca 80, T 3123 2021), in and around Centro.

For full addresses and room rates, see Resources.

Dear Reader, books by Phaidon are recognized worldwide for their beauty, scholarship and elegance. We invite you to return this card with your name and e-mail address so that we can keep you informed of our new publications, special offers and events. Alternatively, visit us at **www.phaidon.com** to see our entire list of books, videos and stationery. Register on-line to be included on our regular e-newsletters.

Subjects in which I have a special interest

☐ General Non-Fiction   ☐ Art   ☐ Photography   ☐ Architecture   ☐ Design

☐ Fashion   ☐ Music   ☐ Children's   ☐ Food   ☐ Travel

Mr/Miss/Ms   Initial   Surname

Name

No./Street

City

Postcode/Zip code   Country

E-mail

This is not an order form. To order please contact Customer Services at the appropriate address overleaf.

Please delete address not required before mailing

PHAIDON PRESS LIMITED

Regent's Wharf

All Saints Street

London N1 9PA

UK

PHAIDON PRESS INC.

180 Varick Street

New York

NY 10014

USA

Return address for USA and Canada only

Return address for UK and countries outside the USA and Canada only

Fasano

This elegant tower signals one of the best hotels in Latin America – as delicious as hot chocolate spiced with cachaça. The Fasano was designed by Márcio Kogan and Isay Weinfeld, and the clubby furniture dotted around the lobby/jazz bar Baretto (see p044) works well with the brick and wood walls. The standard rooms are huge, let alone the Deluxe ones (overleaf). All guests are provided with a butler, so pack your best underwear. It's the service that impresses most: staff remember you by name and have been known to cross town to find lost phones before being asked. The group owns some of the city's top eateries and a stay here helps with reservations, especially useful at Parigi (T 3167 1575), São Paulo's most muscular power-lunch spot. *Rua Vittorio Fasano 88, T 3896 4077, www.fasano.com.br*

Deluxe Room, Fasano

Grand Hyatt

Not so long ago there was little reason to visit the Morumbi/Pinheiros area, but this rapidly developing business district south-west of the city is attracting corporate chains to a location where the São Paulo traffic is not an issue. For those whose main priority is shuttling to and from the office, the Grand Hyatt is the best choice. The standard Grand Queen and King Guest Rooms (above) are par for the course, but at least the lobby/wine bar/lounge (opposite) does try to work a little harder than is usual for a business behemoth. There are some nice touches: a wall of wine bottles offering 2,500 tipples, pink sofas in the public areas and 'jetlag-reduction' treatments, among others, in the Amanary Spa. *Avenida das Nações Unidas 13301, T 2838 1234, www.saopaulo.grand.hyatt.com*

Tivoli Mofarrej

This 220-room outlet of the Portuguese chain Tivoli lacks the intimacy of the high-end boutiques, but it's a smart alternative in a great location. It was renovated in 2009 by Brazilian designer Patricia Anastassiadis in a contemporary style. The Narã Bar and Lounge is enclosed within a glass atrium and has a poolside terrace, where skyscrapers provide a striking backdrop. Chef Sergi Arola serves up sophisticated tapas in Restaurante Arola Vintetres on the 23rd floor, and the Elements Spa by Banyan Tree has 10 treatment rooms with private saunas. Collection Plus rooms are notable for their huge walk-in showers, but high rollers should book the 750 sq m Mofarrej Presidential Suite (above).

Alameda Santos 1437, T 3146 5900, www.tivolihotels.com

L'Hotel

This is a neat boutique hotel that eschews contemporary design in favour of a more rococo feel – think tapestries, Louis XVI chests, Regency chairs and Persian rugs – as seen in the lobby (above). With only 73 rooms on 15 floors, it provides a contrast to the city's many hotel towers. Reputedly inspired by its Parisian namesake, L'Hotel attracts an older international clientele and the type of rich Paulistanos for whom Spanish bedlinen and Italian marble bathrooms carry a certain cachet. The service is very attentive, and the address means it's very convenient for Avenida Paulista as well as MASP (see p066). *Alameda Campinas 266, T 2183 0500, www.portobay.com*

Maksoud Plaza

Not so long ago, the Maksoud was the only top-flight place to stay in São Paulo. Its Presidential Suite has hosted Frank Sinatra, who also sang at the hotel, and Mick Jagger. Considering its great location off Avenida Paulista, it's a wonder how it hasn't been revamped as a shopping mall or office block. Once it was big and swaggering and its staff had a reputation for a certain hauteur, but now, despite major refurbishment, the Maksoud has a faded kitsch glamour all of its own. Its 22-storey atrium (above), complete with fountains, hanging gardens, sculptures, shopping arcade, restaurants, bars and four panoramic lifts, is more 1970s than an Yves Saint Laurent jumpsuit; it's almost worth a visit in itself.
Alameda Campinas 150, T 3145 8000, www.maksoud.com.br

Emiliano

The city's first great luxury hotel, designed by Arthur de Mattos Casas, is light, bright and elegant, and has a younger spirit than the Fasano (see p017). The lobby and bar feature the Campana brothers' 'Azul' chairs and wooden armchairs by José Zanine Caldas, the suites have Eames furniture and the bathroom sinks are carved from Carrara marble. In the Deluxe Rooms (above), the impressive audio and video systems are controlled by a phone touchpad. Everyone gets a butler, but the spacious Suite 1801 is the one to reserve if you plan to entertain. The spa, with its latticework glass wall, offers great views while you relax, and the traffic-beating airport transfers to and from the helipad (opposite) take 20 minutes.

Rua Oscar Freire 384, T 3068 4393,
www.emiliano.com.br

Hilton Morumbi

Opening within a month of the Grand Hyatt (see p020), also in Morumbi, in 2002, the Hilton was a further sign that the chains weren't about to let the boutiques win over their customers without a fight. The executive rooms have a separate check-in and complimentary bar, and while the Canvas Bar & Grill is designed for power lunching, it tries to add flair, with art hanging from the ceiling. The reception area (above) and standard rooms are better than those found in the regular chains, with some nice contemporary touches. A key feature is the luxe pampering offered in the hotel's LivingWell Health Club and Spa. *Avenida das Nações Unidas 12901, T 2845 0000, www.hilton.com*

Hotel Unique

The most theatrical of São Paulo's three major design hotels has smaller rooms than the others and is situated near Ibirapuera Park. Architect Ruy Ohtake's design means that the suites at either end of the corridors lose floor space to the building's distinctive curve (overleaf). Gadgetry is everywhere, from the electric window shutters to the folding glass wall dividing the bathroom from the bedroom and TV, which you can watch as you soak. The Alexandre Herchcovitch-attired staff are friendly without being intrusive and the bar in the lobby (above) is a wine lover's dream, but the best feature is the rooftop Skye Bar (T 3055 4702). Its swimming pool, glass walls and great views attract a chic crowd. *Avenida Brigadeiro Luís Antônio 4700, T 3055 4710, www.hotelunique.com.br*

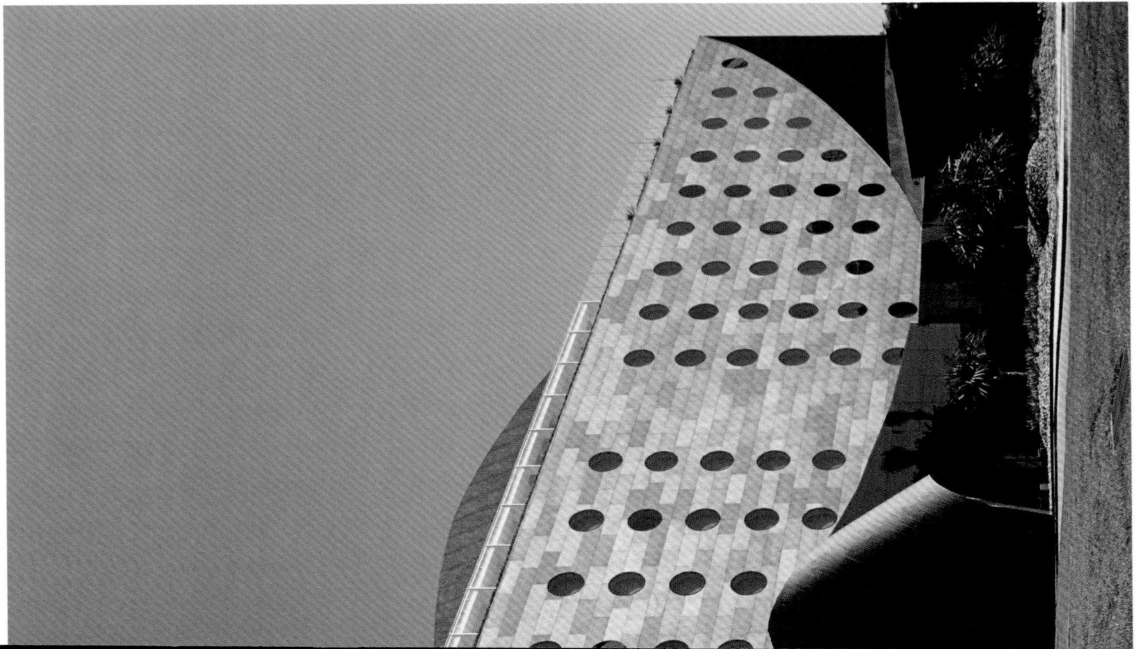

24 HOURS

SEE THE BEST OF THE CITY IN JUST ONE DAY

São Paulo is simultaneously intimidating and stimulating. It doesn't take too long for the first sensation to wear off and you will quickly find yourself in an urban wonderland of culture and creativity. It's impossible to fit all the city's delights into one day, so stick to a tight area, in and around Centro or Jardins, for example. Then you'll be able to experience the best of São Paulo – modernist architecture and design, cutting-edge contemporary art and music, ethnically diverse cuisine and, of course, coffee, which provided the funds to turn the city into one of the world's truly great destinations – without being stuck too long in its worst, the traffic.

Get off to a fighting start with a fresh tropical juice and some *pão de queijo* (cheese bread), perhaps at Café Floresta in Edifício Copan (see p012). Take in a little culture at the Museu da Imagem e do Som (Avenida Europa 158, T 2117 4777), which celebrates Brazilian film and music, or the contemporary art museum MASP (see p066). Have lunch in Dalva e Dito (see p036) before reviewing the oeuvre of legendary Brazilian artist Tomie Ohtake (see p037) in an arresting building designed by her son, Ruy. In the evening you are spoilt for choice. Dine at KAÁ (see p045) or Rodeio (see p058) before drinks and dancing at any number of world-class clubs full of stylish patrons – a scene that Paulistanos believe makes theirs a classier party city than that brash Rio up the coast.

For full addresses, see Resources.

11.00 Mercado Municipal

Almost every street in São Paulo has a caffeine pit stop, but if you want to linger over your first hit of the day, you can't go wrong with the Santo Grão (T 3082 9969) outlet in Rua Oscar Freire. From here, make your way to the Mercado Municipal, a secular cathedral to the city's dominance as one of the world's largest agricultural producers. Designed by Felisberto Ranzini and completed in 1933, the market building is a neo-Gothic and Romanesque jumble, but the Conrad Sorgenicht Filho stained-glass windows are worth a look. Other sights include whole cords of raw tobacco or bits of pig you didn't know were edible. The cheeses and olives make good buys. *Rua da Cantareira 306, T 3228 0673, www.mercadomunicipal.com.br*

1116

12.00 Espaço Havaianas

Colourful, rubber-soled Havaiana flip-flops have become a global phenomenon and this 300 sq m flagship designed by Isay Weinfeld is the best place to stock up. The concrete box is flooded with light, thanks to the large skylights and an interface to the street, which makes the store feel like a public square. The double-height retail area bursts with colour – the complete Havaianas collection is arranged as if in a Pantone book. Rustic elements, such as a tree trunk used as a bench, contrast with the contemporary backdrop, and clever ideas abound – a shipping container displays designs made for overseas markets. Mix and match soles and straps, and choose from hundreds of trinkets and embellishments to make your pair unique.
Rua Oscar Freire 1116, T 3079 3415, www.havaianas.com.br

13.30 Dalva e Dito

In 2009, Brazil's most famous chef, Alex Atala, teamed up with Alain Poletto to launch Dalva e Dito, a less formal, though still pricey follow-up to DOM (see p050). The restaurant specialises in roast meats and down-home Brazilian dishes with artful twists, including interesting takes on traditional snacks such as *bolinhos de mandioca* (fried yuca balls) and *carne seca* (dried meat), prepared in a state-of-the-art display kitchen. The welcoming room features handmade wood tables recycled from the flooring, childlike murals, a charming outdoor space and Athos Bulcão tile designs that complement the traditional blue-and-white crockery from Porcelana Monte Sião in Minas Gerais. The downstairs bar (above) attracts well-to-do locals.
Rua Padre João Manuel 1115, T 3068 4444, www.dalvaedito.com.br

17.30 Instituto Tomie Ohtake

Tomie Ohtake, the mother of architect Ruy, is one of Brazil's greatest artists. This institute, whose director happens to be another son, Ricardo, is a must, for Tomie's spare abstract paintings and engravings displayed within 7,500 sq m of exhibition space, and Ruy's strikingly playful blue and mauve building. The complex, which also comprises the 22-storey Torre Faria Lima and the inverted trapezoid of Torre Pedrosa de Moraes (above right), was built between 1998 and 2004, and its odd shapes and bright colours continue to polarise public opinion. After visiting, explore the funky boutiques, galleries and boho bars and restaurants in nearby Vila Madalena, or if it's the weekend, take a stroll to the Praça Benedito Calixto fleamarket.
Avenida Faria Lima 201, T 2245 1900, www.institutotomieohtake.org.br

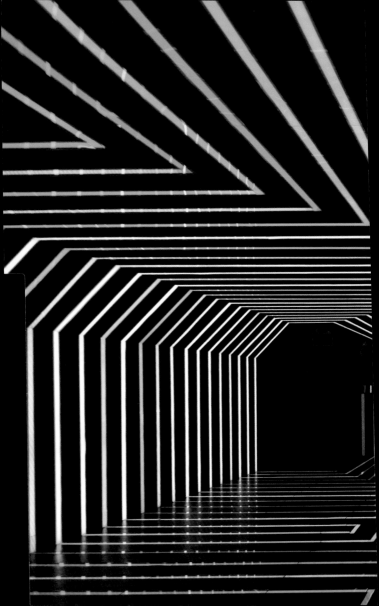

11.45 D-Edge
The pulsing D-Edge is a must on a week
night, in part for its LED lighting system,
generated by beat recognition and audio
software. In 2010, owner/DJ Renato Ratier
expanded the club, with original designer
Muti Randolph again in charge. The Veuve
Clicquot Lounge boasts leather seating
and Ferro wood panelling, and there's
a spacious terrace with fantastic views.
Alameda Olga 170, T 3667 8334

URBAN LIFE
CAFÉS, RESTAURANTS, BARS AND NIGHTCLUBS

Paulistanos are proud that their city has the most sophisticated nightlife in South America – and we mean *night* life. The prime dinner reservation is for 9pm or later, and neither the chic lounges of Jardins nor the boho bars of Vila Madalena get going until midnight. This relentless scene, which can be shockingly expensive, has enough superb options to keep you interested for weeks. But you can also do São Paulo on a budget, from the humble *yakitori* shacks of Liberdade ('Little Tokyo') to the guarana street stalls and the delicious fruit juices (*bacuri, açaí* or *cupuaçu*) in the *suco* bars.

The restaurant scene is shaped by the city's immigrant history, and boasts outstanding examples of international cuisine – Italian at Fasano (see p060); Japanese at Kinoshita (Rua Jacques Félix 405, T 3849 6940) and sushi-fusion at Jun Sakamoto (Rua Lisboa 55, T 3088 6019); Lebanese at Arábia (Rua Haddock Lobo 1397, T 3061 2203); and Spanish at Clos de Tapas (see p051) and Adega Santiago (Rua Sampaio Vidal 1072, T 3081 5211). Brazilian chef Alex Atala (see p036) has also inspired a revitalisation of domestic cuisine, for example at Mocotó (Avenida Nossa Senhora do Loreto 1100, T 2951 3056), which specialises in dishes from the north-east. Afterwards, dance it off in one of the dynamic clubs – Lions (Avenida Brigadeiro Luís Antônio 277, T 3104 7157), D-Edge (see p038) and Disco (Rua Atílio Innocenti 160, T 3078 0404) are the guest lists to target. *For full addresses, see Resources.*

Kosushi

Jun Sakamoto's eponymous restaurant has a reputation for the best Japanese food in the city, but Kosushi chef George Yuji Koshoji is not far behind – many of his sashimi innovations have been copied by his rivals. The success of the original venue on Rua Viradouro (T 3167 7272) led to the opening of this second location in Cidade Jardim, both designed by architect Arthur de Mattos Casas. The illuminated ceiling in the sushi bar area creates an intimate feel, whereas the dining room is better for groups and features a communal table lit by a cluster of Tom Dixon Beat Series lamps (above). Portraits of ordinary Japanese shot by Brazilian fashion designer Alexandre Herchcovitch decorate a wonderfully understated contemporary space.
Shopping Cidade Jardim, T 3552 7272, www.kosushi.com.br

Forneria Villa Daslu

The third branch of Forneria, the excellent upmarket *sanduicheria* concept, opened in 2009 in the retail temple Villa Daslu. Its more formal feel was created by Marcio Kogan, and features Tom Dixon lights, leather 'Series 7' chairs by Arne Jacobsen and a delightful collection of 1950s and 1960s clocks by George Nelson for Vitra. There's a range of meat and fish dishes, yet it maintains its roots in superb pastas and sandwiches. It's only open for weekend brunch, but the original outlet, Forneria San Paulo on Rua Amauri (T 3078 0099), remains a great option on any day. Here, Isay Weinfeld mixed rich woods, foliage and clean lines, and in 2010 designed an additional outdoor space bounded by textured stone walls with a water feature. *Avenida Chedid Jafet 131, T 3841 9680, www.forneria.com.br*

Baretto

The bar attached to the lobby of the Fasano hotel (see p017) is as cosy and warming as a single malt. The English club-style furniture, discreet lighting and décor are a contemporary take on a 1930s cocktail lounge, and the house band, the Mario Edson Trio, has been entertaining Paulistanos for decades. Their repertoire of jazz and bossa nova standards is smoother than a silk bag full of velvet,

and on Thursdays, Fridays and Saturdays, singer Ana Cañas adds a seductive swing. Guest stars also appear regularly. The caipirinhas are mixed with *Nega Fulô*, oak-aged cachaça that's mostly exported. *Rua Vittorio Fasano 88, T 3896 4000, www.fasano.com.br*

KAÁ

Designed by Arthur Casas, KAÁ is an impressive addition to the restaurant scene. An unassuming white stucco façade hides a lush, dramatic space that transports visitors from the metropolitan chaos into a high-ceilinged, 700 sq m sanctuary. The highlight is an elongated garden wall (above), covered with species from the Atlantic rainforest, which seamlessly blends indoor and outdoor environments, helped by the retractable canvas roof. Dishes such as brie tortellini with fig compote, and ravioli of foie gras with truffle oil are staples of the French/ Italian menu, created by chefs Pascal Valero and Paulo Barroso de Barros. In the mezzanine cocktail lounge, DJs belt out tracks for the Paulista jet set.

Avenida Presidente Juscelino Kubitschek 279, T 3045 0043, kaarestaurante.com.br

Spot

Dwarfed by the high-rise office blocks just off Avenida Paulista, this little villa stands out, partly for its menu of fashionable European and Asian fusion food and partly because of the cool crowd of media and design types that it has been attracting for years. It's relatively staid at lunchtimes, when local business folk on expenses proliferate. It's at night when the place comes into its own, and the banquettes become crowded and noisy, packed with models, actors and musicians out to see and be seen – a crowd-pulling trick that works equally well in the owners' hamburger joint Ritz (T 3062 5830), in Jardins. At Spot, opt for a table by the window on the left as you enter, so that you can watch the fountains in the plaza outside.

Alameda Ministro Rocha Azevedo 72, T 3284 6131, www.restaurantespot.com.br

Nbox

Tapas has become a major culinary trend in São Paulo, and restaurant/bar Nbox has jumped on the bandwagon. It does so with a whimsical tongue-in-cheek eclecticism, by packing Paulistanos into a stack of 12 metal cargo boxes for cocktails, Iberian classics such as ham croquettes and *gambas a la plancha*, and the odd live performance. There is plenty of volume in the main seating area and skylights are employed elsewhere, but you may find it a challenge to pass an entire evening here – Nbox is luxurious for a shipping container, but lacks the understated style so easy to find in this city. Built as a pop-up addition to a vacant lot in Jardim América, it is scheduled to ship out in 2011 but there is no firm date yet, so call ahead.
Avenida São Gabriel 600, T 7711 5655, www.nbox.art.br

DOM

A fixture on lists of the world's 50 best restaurants, DOM is run by TV celebrity chef Alex Atala, who reinterprets Brazilian staples – cod, black beans, *farofa* (flour made from cassava) – with a French twist. In 2010, designer José Roberto Moreira do Valle reimagined the restaurant for its 10th anniversary, creating an elegant space that features high-backed, linen-covered sofas, wooden animal sculptures and a Baccarat chandelier by Philippe Starck. The dining room has now caught up with a decade of evolution in the kitchen, and the clientele is a mix of the rich, the famous and those splashing out on a special occasion. There are two tasting menus (R$280 and R$400), but it's the wine prices that will make your eyes water. *Rua Barão de Capanema 549, T 3088 0761, www.domrestaurante.com.br*

Clos de Tapas

We tend to be cautious about fusion, but at Clos, the Spanish tapas with a Brazilian twist is done to perfection. Owner Marcelo Fernandez launched the venture in 2011 down the block from his Japanese eaterie Kinoshita (see p040), one of São Paulo's finest. Brazilian chef Ligia Karazawa and Spaniard Raúl Jímenez trained at elBulli, and the duo conjure up small plates such as baby pork with *graviola* (soursop) and radish, and duck foie gras with *tucupi* (cassava root extract). Local architect Naoki Otake designed the two-storey glass-fronted box, which features native wood and weathered steel and is dominated by a rock wall decorated with artwork by Chilean Enrique Rodríguez. The garden was landscaped by Gilberto Elkis.
Rua Domingos Fernandes 548,
T 3045 2154, www.closdetapas.com.br

Sonique Bar
This lounge/club opened in 2009 and is typically packed with GLS – *gays, lesbicas e simpatizantes*. While the vibe is warm and fuzzy, Triptyque's ironic rococo design has a raw feel, from the concrete façade to the voluminous main space, where 10m cinderblock walls are dressed with French-style moulding, shapes that are replicated in neon on the ceiling.
Rua Bela Cintra 461, T 2628 8707

Número

Nightlife impresarios Marcos Campos and Fernanda Barbosa teamed up in 2010 to launch Número, another hot little number designed by Isay Weinfeld, who squeezed this sexy restaurant/cocktail lounge into a parcel just 5m wide but 61m deep. The space consists of a series of beautifully lit 'living rooms' separated by steps and filled with custom-made leather sofas. Visible through the plate-glass back wall is a lush garden, more apparent from the colourful club space downstairs. Dishes such as beef stroganoff and crab cakes are staples of chefs Victor Vasconcellos and Adriana Cymes' international menu. The building's façade (opposite) features an intricate pattern of numbers in varying fonts, laser-cut from naval wood.
Rua da Consolação 3585, T 3061 3995, www.barnumero.com.br

Bar Volt

When the city banned 'visual pollution' in 2007, bar impresario Facundo Guerra saw an opportunity. Two-and-a-half years later, with the collaboration of visual artist Kleber Matheus and architect Eduardo Chalabi, he opened Volt, decorated with salvaged neon from the 1970s onwards, collected from the façades of the bars in the district of Rio Augusta. Located in a 400 sq m warehouse, Volt also features a mirrored wall, a patio with a vertical garden and Eames chairs. The lighting itself, including new designs by Matheus, is all for sale and changes periodically according to themes. The result is a vibrant space full of energy. Volt is famous for its cocktails, although they come at a price. The tropical take on the margarita is popular, and uses a reduction of ginger and passion fruit juice instead of lemon. *Rua Haddock Lobo 40, T 2936 4041, www.barvolt.com.br*

Rodeio

It is something of an understatement
to say there's no shortage of great places
to eat meat in São Paulo, as *churrascarias*
(barbecue restaurants) are the city's USP.
Choose between the justly famous Baby
Beef Rubaiyat (T 3165 8888), where the
beef comes from the owners' ranch, and
Barbacoa (T 3168 5522), in which nine
different cuts of beef, still dripping from
the grill, just keep coming until you pop.

But at Rodeio, there's something about
the *picanha* (top sirloin rolled in salt
and garlic with a thick cap of fat) that
keeps pulling us back. Sunday is the best
time to visit, when the various dining
rooms and intimate bar area (above) are
packed with high-powered Paulistanos
brunching with families and friends.
*Rua Haddock Lobo 1498, T 3474 1333,
www.rodeiosp.com.br*

Lorena 1989

This hip restaurant is the brainchild of the French-Brazilian collective Surface to Air. The protagonists, David Laloum, Karina Motta, Rafael Pelosini and Sebastian Orth, designed the space themselves, giving it a certain rustic chic with painted brick walls, farmhouse-style furniture and wooden beams, as well as unique touches such as rope lamps designed by Orth. Chef Leo Botto's Mediterranean-Italian menu includes many dishes prepared in a wood-fired oven. Request a table on the veranda, the most sceney spot, and a jug of sangria, the house speciality. Surface to Air also runs Bar Secreto (Rua Álvaro Anes 97), where Madonna once threw an after-party. *Alameda Lorena 1989, T 3081 2966, www.lorena1989.com.br*

Restaurante Fasano
Since 1982, this temple to modern Italian cuisine has been setting the standard for all other restaurants in São Paulo. Its 2003 move to Isay Weinfeld's dark, dramatic space on the ground floor of the Fasano family's hotel (see p017) only made it an even hotter ticket. The menu draws on various Italian regions. *Rua Vittorio Fasano 88, T 3062 4000, www.fasano.com.br*

INSIDER'S GUIDE

MELANIE BITTI, MODEL AND STYLIST

Long-time Jardins resident Melanie Bitti often starts the day with a strong *cafezinho* at her local bakery Saint Germain Panificadora Confeitaria (Rua Manuel Guedes 110, T 3167 5400), where there is live music during brunch at weekends. For lunch she might pop into the happening Mani (Rua Joaquim Antunes 210, T 3085 4148), which is popular for its courtyard dining and Brazilian fare, or Ici Bistro (Rua Pará 36, T 3259 6896), for its excellent French food and location in Higienópolis. 'It's a lovely area, full of trees and beautiful buildings,' she says. A favourite spot for afternoon coffee and *doces* (sweet treats) is Dulca (Rua Oscar Freire 778, T 2769 9003). 'The streetside tables are always buzzing.'

Bitti says she's addicted to NK Store (Rua Sarandi 34, T 3897 2600) and is a fan of the elegant modern chic of Brazilian designer Andrea Marques (Sala 22, Rua Joaquim Antunes 177, T 2537 6605). 'I like art, and especially photography,' she says. 'They have great shows at Galeria Leme (Rua Agostinho Cantu 88, T 3814 8184).'

In the evening, Bitti likes to dine at Arturito (Rua Artur de Azevedo 542, T 3063 4951), a hip restaurant known for its classic dishes as well as unexpected menu choices, such as sweetbreads. Nagayama (Rua Bandeira Paulista 369, T 3079 4675) is her top recommendation for sushi. Later, she likes to drop in for drinks at Número (see p054), for its 'comfy sofas and gorgeous design'. *For full addresses, see Resources.*

ARCHITOUR
A GUIDE TO SÃO PAULO'S ICONIC BUILDINGS

As befits a city proud of its work ethic and unabashed about its worship of mammon, São Paulo is more concerned about issues of production, consumption and its ever-growing population than it is with preservation. The distant past has little place in a city committed so heavily to the here and now. And it shows: only a few of the coffee baron mansions put up on Avenida Paulista in the 1890s made it through the building boom of the 1960s.

As for buildings from further back in Brazil's colonial past, almost all have gone. Two of the city's most historic structures, the Páteo do Collégio mission (Praça Páteo do Collégio, T 3105 6898), in which the Jesuits christened the city, and the house where Emperor Dom Pedro declared Brazil's independence from the Portuguese in 1822, are mere replicas of the originals.

What the city does have in abundance is Latin America's finest collection of modernist buildings: visit São Paulo's first skyscraper, the 1929 Edifício Martinelli (Avenida São João 35, T 3104 2477); Oswaldo Bratke's sleek, elegant 1950 Fundação Oscar Americano (Avenida Morumbi 4077, T 3742 0077); and Franz Heep's towering 1965 Edifício Itália (Avenida Ipiranga 344, T 3257 3953). All this, and the work of brutalists such as Paulo Mendes da Rocha (opposite), Lina Bo Bardi (see p078) and Rino Levi, almost makes you glad Paulistanos haven't been more conservation-minded.

For full addresses, see Resources.

Museu Brasileiro de Escultura (MuBE)

In 1986, Paulo Mendes da Rocha won a competition to design Brazil's national sculpture museum by producing not so much a building as a series of interlocking brutalist slabs, which shape the museum out of the spaces they create. In so doing, they reinvent the surrounding landscape. The 7,000 sq m triangular site is on a main thoroughfare linking the Jardim Europa residential district to the city centre. Da Rocha treated the museum and landscape as a whole – the large concrete slabs create partly underground internal spaces and also form the exterior plaza. Despite its complex design, the individual forms are simple, and a 60m-long, 12m-wide beam (above) frames the museum, making a kind of porch.

Avenida Europa 218, T 2594 2601, www.mube.art.br

Museu de Arte de São Paulo (MASP)

Lina Bo Bardi, a member of the Italian Communist Party during WWII, left Italy for Brazil in 1946. Although she also worked in Rio and Salvador, she will always be associated with São Paulo, where she died in 1992. Her brutalist art box, designed in 1957 and opened in 1968, squats among the skyscrapers on Avenida Paulista, where it seems to be floating on two wraparound red columns. Inside is Latin America's best collection of European art – a testimony to the purchasing power of the coffee barons who once lived on the boulevard and of the arm-twisting power of Bardi's husband, Pietro Maria, who built most of the collection. There are good early Picassos, a Degas or two and amusing works by Bosch. It also has a good canteen. *Avenida Paulista 1578, T 3251 5644, www.masp.art.br*

Edifício Bretagne

There are many splendid buildings in Higienópolis. Stroll along its leafy streets and take in such temples to modernity as Franz Heep's Edifício Lausanne or his Lugano Locarno apartment tower; Vilanova Artigas' Edifício Louveira (see p076) or Rino Levi and Cerqueira Cesar's Edifício Prudência at Avenida Higienópolis 265. For a change of style, take in the gothic chocolate box that is the Vila Maria. At the corner of Avenida Higienópolis and Rua Dona Veridiana, it houses the São Paulo Club. Another building that really stands out is João Artacho Jurado's Bretagne (opposite), which is quite simply one of the world's great addresses. This 1950s fun palace is a riot – from the boudoir furniture in the lobby to the fanciful friezes on the ceilings and the residents-only bar in the basement; inveigle an invite to see what modern living should be all about.
Avenida Higienópolis 938

Faculdade de Arquitetura e Urbanismo

Architect/professor João Batista Vilanova Artigas had as much influence as Paulo Mendes da Rocha in the development of Brazilian brutalism. Not only did he design this 1961 university faculty building, he also developed the curriculum. A series of suspended cast-concrete boxes house studios, classrooms and lecture halls, and overlook a voluminous public space drenched in light that filters in through translucent panes in the 60m-span roof. The structure recalls the work of Artigas' mentor, the Russian modernist Gregori Warchavchik. In the grounds, an ancient-Greek-style auditorium is used for talks and performances. Garden design is rarely overlooked in Brazil and the landscaping brings tropical charm and a sense of place to this concrete behemoth.
Rua Lago 876, T 3031 2552, www.fau.usp.br

Rui Barbosa Courthouse

Architect Decio Tozzi's civic justice building consolidated São Paulo's courts in one space in 2004. The design is based on the idea of transparency – a concept sadly lacking in the Brazilian system, and, ironically, there was a scandal over the redirection of R$170m in construction funds to politicians involved in the project. The highlight is a glass-enclosed 'public square', which is a jaw-dropping 72m tall and 50m wide (opposite). Within this atrium is a restaurant and auditorium that features artwork by Tozzi's brother, Claudio. It is surrounded by a series of ramps and walkways that traffics more than 20,000 people per day to the administrative and judicial areas. There are also 20 high-speed elevators – four reserved for judges only, bringing a new meaning to swift justice.
Avenida Marquês de São Vicente 235

Auditório Ibirapuera
Oscar Niemeyer and Roberto Burle
Marx's Ibirapuera Park project was,
for decades, one of the great 'what-ifs'
of world architecture, but their vision
for a modernist Central Park was finally
completed in 2005, with the construction
of Niemeyer's white, wedge-shaped
music auditorium. The park has a great
atmosphere on weekends and holidays.
República do Líbano/Quarto Centenário

Edifício Louveira

In the 1940s and early 1950s, the tree-lined streets of Higienópolis rattled to the sound of apartment building for the bourgeoisie. One of the architectural pioneers was Vilanova Artigas, originally influenced by Frank Lloyd Wright, who championed spatial continuity and changes of levels, through the creation of great voids and mezzanines linked by slopes, to dramatic effect on the Edifício Louveira in 1946. He set a trend by bringing in the artist Francisco 'Rebolo' Gonsales to paint murals that brighten the building, and his use of colour and window shuttering brought tropical modern style to the area. Artigas went on to design many of São Paulo's important brutalist structures, such as the Faculdade de Arquitetura e Urbanismo (see p070), before being sidelined because of his leftist beliefs during the military dictatorship.
Praça Vilaboim

Caṣa de Vidro
Lina Bo Bardi's Glass House was built
among the Mata Atlântica rainforest,
most of which was later cleared to create
the fashionable suburb of Morumbi,
although dense vegetation remains as
the garden. Built in 1950-51, it was Bo
Bardi's first construction and she lived
in it until her death. It's now attached
to an institute dedicated to her work.
Rua General Almério de Moura 200

SHOPPING
THE BEST RETAIL THERAPY AND WHAT TO BUY

The shopping in *Sampa* deserves to be mentioned in the same breath as Paris or New York. There's great design talent here, matched with great purchasing power. Malls are not the sterile places found in the US, cases in point being Cidade Jardim, a beautiful space designed by Arthur Casas, and an eagerly anticipated second Iguatemi (Avenida Presidente Juscelino Kubitschek 2041), opened in 2011, housing a reinvented Daslu, which has morphed into a fashion brand. Or head to Rua Oscar Freire for independent boutiques by domestic names, such as Adriana Barra (see p086).

Galleries such as Mendes Wood (Rua da Consolação 3368, T 2528 6331) and Vermelho (Rua Minas Gerais 350, T 3138 1520) promote a pool of talented artists, while Choque Cultural (Rua João Moura 997, T 3061 4051) sells cutting-edge urban art. Out of the seemingly limitless interiors options, try Cool Life (Rua da Consolação 3589, T 3062 5958), Interni (Alameda Gabriel Monteiro da Silva 1022, T 3081 1664) and Forma (Avenida Cidade Jardim 924, T 3816 7233), housed in an arresting box designed in 1987 by Mendes da Rocha. For antiques, visit Filter (Rua Prof Rubião Meira 36, T 3085 2239) and Ricardo Varuzza (Rua João Moura 499, T 3898 0458), which has famous Brazilian pieces and infamous pricing. Livraria da Vila (see p085) is an excellent one-stop shop for a fascinating selection of art and design books, and that Brazilian must-buy – music. *For full addresses, see Resources.*

Galeria Melissa

The words 'shoe shop' don't really do Galeria Melissa justice. Muti Randolph, interior designer for D-Edge (see p038), reworks the shop and entrance every three months. Installations have included everything from murals by artist Kleber Matheus to sculpture by the Campana Brothers and a collage of half-a-million Post-it notes displaying messages written by passersby. The concept keeps Melissa fresh, especially for patrons of the Dulca (see p062) café over the road, who get a grandstand view. Inside, funky bubble stands exhibit Melissa's many rubber-made creations, designed by the likes of Karim Rashid and Vivienne Westwood. *Rua Oscar Freire 827, T 3083 3612, www.melissa.com.br*

Micasa Volume B

Marcio Kogan's Vitra showroom is meant to have a work-in-progress feel, but it is too gorgeous to pull it off. The brutalist concrete building has an extraordinarily rough, articulated texture, which creates a dramatic effect when lit up at night. Inside, a backlit ceiling casts light down unfinished bare-concrete walls, while layers of iron rebar form brises-soleil at the rear. Volume B is an annexe to interiors store Micasa, which launched in 2007 and was created by local architects Triptyque. It carries global brands, from the Eameses to Established & Sons, as well as talented Brazilian designers such as Zanini de Zanine, Marcelo Rosenbaum and Felipe Protti. It also serves as an event space for the store's frequent happenings.
Rua Estados Unidos 2109, T 3088 1238, www.micasa.com.br/volumeb

Forum

Even among the many sleek stores along Rua Oscar Freire, Forum manages to stand out. Isay Weinfeld's mixture of cool contemporary design and tactile, raw, indigenous Brazilian materials has turned Forum into a kind of theatre to shopping, complete with a coloured-glass mosaic staircase for making a show-stopping entrance. At the top of the stairs is a bar and wall made from Brazilian wood, vines and mud. Elsewhere, around the angular space – only minimally occupied by clothes and shoes – are a handmade carpet of Brazilian fabric, cowhide stools and untreated wood tables. Hemp, rattan and bamboo also make an appearance. This is worth a visit for the building as much as it is for the clothes, which are rather fine. *Rua Oscar Freire 916, T 3085 6269, www.forum.com.br*

Livraria da Vila

Brazilians love their bookshops, and at Livraria da Vila you can see why. The store is recognisable for its metal display-case doors that pivot 90 degrees to serve as a permeable boundary. It's a clever concept by Isay Weinfeld, who placed the showpiece entrance in an otherwise minimal concrete façade. Inside, a narrow private home has been transformed and opened up, and features cut-out spaces between floors lined with books. Author readings, musical performances and other events are held in the first-floor café. There is also a 2,400 sq m branch of Livraria da Vila (T 3755 5811) in the Cidade Jardim mall, featuring a striking yellow staircase, darkwood shelves and a floating, glass-walled auditorium. *Alameda Lorena 1731, T 3062 1063, www.livrariadavila.com.br*

Adriana Barra

Fashion designer Adriana Barra's womenswear is wildly popular in Brazil for its graphic, boho chic and cheeky, irreverent tone, and she has now branched out into childrenswear, home and office furnishings. This conceptual store is inspired by a 'cosmopolitan beach hotel' and opened in 2010 in a period townhouse. You enter through a 'lobby', complete with a concierge desk and a brass luggage cart from which hang highlights from her collection. Dressing rooms are reminiscent of saunas, and coffee and snacks are served in a kitchen adorned with ceramic tiles designed by Barra for interiors brand Jatobá. To cap it all off, the charming multilingual staff wear hotel name tags. *Alameda Franca 1243, T 2925 2300, www.adrianabarra.com.br*

SPORTS AND SPAS
WORK OUT, CHILL OUT OR JUST WATCH

For all its Formula One racing drivers, tennis players and beach volleyball stars, the sport that most defines the Brazilian way of life is football. On the world stage it is synonymous with outrageous flair, flowing moves and, until recently, an admirably lackadaisical approach to work rate and defence. At home, the picture is a little different, and the Brazilian game has major problems. It exports more of its young stars than any country in the world; intermittent violence and traffic jams have taken their toll on attendances; most clubs have huge debts; a bewildering array of cups and championships exhausts the players and devalues matches; and the incredible pressure for results means that the major teams often replace managers three or even four times a season. That said, the chance to attend a local derby, such as Corinthians versus Palmeiras or São Paulo FC, should not be missed.

Amateur sportspeople go head to head at the many prestigious private clubs, such as Harmonia de Tênis (Rua Canadá 658, T 3087 0533) and Iate Clube de Santos (Avenida Higienópolis 18, T 3155 4400); you'll need to befriend a local to get in. A far more accessible way to work up a sweat is a run or bike ride through Ibirapuera Park (see p074). Once the preserve of the top hotels, the luxury pampering industry is currently booming in Brazil, and you can't go wrong with the spa at Cidade Jardim (see p090). *For full addresses, see Resources.*

SESC Fábrica da Pompéia

Work out in an architectural gem by cadging an invite from a member of the SESC, a quasi trade union that runs several of the city's community centres. The one to blag entry to is Lina Bo Bardi's vast ex-refrigeration plant (above) on Rua Clélia. It has a pool, gym, three sports halls, six multipurpose courts and four fitness rooms. Bo Bardi added two stark towers connected by triangular walkways to turn this into a 12,000 sq m modernist space of rawness and power. The shorter tower, which houses the gym, has a series of odd-shaped windows. The cavernous rooms are also home to a beer hall, restaurant, library and theatre. Best of all, SESC is used by a real cross-section of people, so you'll meet all sorts. *Rua Clélia 93, T 3871 7700, www.sescsp.org.br*

Spa Cidade Jardim

This excellent spa is located on the fifth floor of the no-expense-spared Cidade Jardim mall. Facilities include a Finnish sauna, Vichy showers, a fitness area with TechnoGym machines and two pools, one with ergometric jets, both with captivating views. Oversized lockers made from Amazon teak provide a local flavour and adjacent 'dressing suites' allow for a dignified experience. Staff job titles include spa therapist, concierge, butler, lifestyle coach and mind and body instructor, and while many might not be of any direct use, their very existence underscores the high-luxe ethos. This, along with the unbeatable post-spa lunch and shopping options here make it perfect for jet-lagged travellers.
Avenida Magalhães de Castro, T 3552 3575, www.shoppingcidadejardimjhsf.com.br

CEU Pimentas
This 16,000 sq m leisure and sports complex designed by architects Biselli + Katchborian has become a centre of gravity and pride in a disadvantaged community not accustomed to such municipal treasures. In a voluminous concrete hangar-like building, the central hall has a smart, colour-coded system that leads along pathways, bridges and stairs to various spaces that include a restaurant, several art, dance and music studios and an auditorium. The impressive sports facility is popular for basketball and five-a-side football, and there's a gym and three swimming pools. CEU is on the way to the airport in Guarulhos – a handy stop-off if you've got a late flight.
Estrada do Caminho Velho 351,
T 2481 6422

Jockey Club
Horseracing in São Paulo dates from
1875, and the *hipódromo*, designed by
Elisário Bahiana and Victor Brecheret,
opened in 1941. It attracts big crowds to
major races (January to April) and also
hosts concerts and events. Watch from
the restaurant Charlô (pictured), as you
sip a cocktail in art nouveau surrounds.
*Avenida Lineu de Paula Machado 1263,
T 2161 8300, www.jockeysp.com.br*

ESCAPES

WHERE TO GO IF YOU WANT TO LEAVE TOWN

A key element in escaping São Paulo is how to get out. If you have a contact with the use of a helicopter, take advantage, as traffic to the coast is intolerable, especially at weekends. Around public holidays, it can take five hours to cover the last 20km. If you must travel by car, leave early: your average hipster Paulistano heads straight from a nightclub in the early hours, drives to the beach and catches up on sleep on the sand. The coast near São Paulo can be divided into that north of Santos, which is more developed with better beaches, and that south of the city, where poor roads and fewer gorgeous beaches mean tourism is less important.

Perhaps one of the most beautiful spots on the coast between Santos and Rio is Ilhabela, a dramatic volcanic isle 20 minutes by ferry from São Sebastião, and the main summer hangout for the wealthy of São Paulo. Further north, about halfway to Rio, is the delightful colonial town of Paraty, a place to indulge in leisurely ambling and boat trips to the local islands and beaches.

North-east of São Paulo, the Mantiqueira mountains serve as a stunning backdrop for horse riding at Haras Polana (Rodovia SP50, Bairro dos Melos, Campos do Jordão, T 12 3664 3313). And if that sounds too strenuous, head to the architectural paradise of Curitiba (opposite) or take a 90-minute flight to Brasilia and neighbouring Goiânia, an absolute must for fans of modernism. *For full addresses, see Resources.*

Curitiba

Once a cowboy town, Curitiba, a five-hour drive south-west of São Paulo in the Serra do Mar mountains, matured into a city after German, Polish, Italian and Ukrainian settlers mobbed the place in the 19th and 20th centuries. Now it's an example of what would happen if architects ruled the world. In the 1960s, local architect and later city mayor, Jaime Lerner, launched a far-reaching urban-planning programme, including radical traffic management, strict building controls and the creation of huge public parks. As a result, Curitiba is one of the cleanest, most efficiently run cities in South America, with exceptional modern architecture, including the Museu Oscar Niemeyer (above, T 41 3350 4400) and the 1992 Ópera de Arame (overleaf, T 41 3355 6072), a steel-tube construction designed by Domingos Bongestabs.

Ópera de Arame, Curitiba

Uxua Casa Hotel, Trancoso

Trancoso is a fishing village in southern Bahia with stunning beaches and that typically Brazilian barefoot-chic vibe. Set among the colourful colonial buildings and charming restaurants, the boutique Uxua Casa Hotel is a collection of 10 beachy villas designed by Wilbert Das, the owner and former creative director of Diesel, who has combined a Bahian design aesthetic with laidback European exclusivity; book the eco-conscious but lavish treehouse Casa da Árvore (above). The luxury hippy feel continues with a spa, a beach lounge, private gardens and an aventurine quartz pool (opposite). It's a two-hour flight to Salvador and then an hour's drive to reach Trancoso. *Quadrado, T 73 3668 2277, www.uxua.com*

Sabina Escola Parque do Conhecimento
The industrial municipality of Santo
André, 15km south-east of São Paulo, is
home to one of Paulo Mendes da Rocha's
more recent works, the Sabina School,
designed in collaboration with local
architects MMBB and opened in 2007.
A simple yet imposing 184m-long, 31m-
wide, white slab of a roof seems to hover
1.5m off the ground, supported by just a
few columns. Hidden windows allow light
into the mainly underground interior, which
includes a science museum and temporary
exhibition spaces (above), while outside
is a mix of public spaces, from gardens
to stone plazas and cycle trails.
Rua Juquiá 135, Santo André, T 4422 2001

NOTES

SKETCHES AND MEMOS

RESOURCES
CITY GUIDE DIRECTORY

A

Adega Santiago 040
Rua Sampaio Vidal 1072
T 3081 5211
www.adegasantiago.com.br

Adriana Barra 086
Alameda Franca 1243
T 2925 2300
www.adrianabarra.com.br

Andrea Marques 062
Sala 22
Rua Joaquim Antunes 177
T 2537 6605
www.andreamarques.com.br

Arábia 040
Rua Haddock Lobo 1397
T 3061 2203
www.arabia.com.br

Arturito 062
Rua Artur de Azevedo 542
T 3063 4951
www.arturito.com.br

Auditório Ibirapuera 074
República do Líbano/Quarto Centenário
www.auditorioibirapuera.com.br

B

Baby Beef Rubaiyat 058
Avenida Faria Lima 2954
T 3165 8888
www.rubaiyat.com.br

Bar da Dona Onça 012
Edifício Copan
Avenida Ipiranga 200
T 3257 2016

Bar Secreto 059
Rua Álvaro Anes 97

Bar Volt 056
Rua Haddock Lobo 40
T 2936 4041
www.barvolt.com.br

Barbacoa 058
Rua Dr Renato Paes de Barros 65
T 3168 5522
www.barbacoa.com.br

Baretto 044
Fasano
Rua Vittorio Fasano 88
T 3896 4000
www.fasano.com.br

C

Café Floresta 032
Edifício Copan
Avenida Ipiranga 200

Casa de Vidro 078
Rua General Almério de Moura 200

CEU Pimentas 092
Estrada do Caminho Velho 351
T 2481 6422

Charlô 094
Jockey Club
Avenida Lineu de Paula Machado 1263
T 3032 4613
www.charlo.com.br

Choque Cultural 080
Rua João Moura 997
T 3061 4051
www.choquecultural.com.br

Clos de Tapas 051
Rua Domingos Fernandes 548
T 3045 2154
www.closdetapas.com.br

Cool Life 080
Rua da Consolação 3589
T 3062 5958
www.coollife.com.br

HOTELS

ADDRESSES AND ROOM RATES

Emiliano 026
Room rates:
double, US$800;
Deluxe Room, US$800;
Suite 1801, US$14,700
Rua Oscar Freire 384
T 3068 4393
www.emiliano.com.br

Fasano 017
Room rates:
double, US$680;
Deluxe Room, US$860
Rua Vittorio Fasano 88
T 3896 4077
www.fasano.com.br

Grand Hyatt 020
Room rates:
double, US$630;
Grand Queen and King Room, US$630
Avenida das Nações Unidas 13301
T 2838 1234
www.saopaulo.grand.hyatt.com

Hilton Morumbi 028
Room rates:
double, US$350
Avenida das Nações Unidas 12901
T 2845 0000
www.hilton.com

L'Hotel 024
Room rates:
double, US$330
Alameda Campinas 266
T 2183 0500
www.portobay.com

Maksoud Plaza 025
Room rates:
double, US$290;
Presidential Suite, US$5,200
Alameda Campinas 150
T 3145 8000
www.maksoud.com.br

Normandie Design Hotel 016
Room rates:
double, US$135
Avenida Ipiranga 1187
T 3311 9855
www.normandiedesign.com.br

Pergamon Hotel 016
Room rates:
double, US$150
Rua Frei Caneca 80
T 3123 2021
www.pergamon.com.br

Renaissance 016
Room rates:
double, US$380
Alameda Santos 2233
T 3069 2233
www.marriott.co.uk

Tivoli Mofarrej 022
Room rates:
double, US$430;
Mofarrej Presidential Suite, $19,940
Alameda Santos 1437
T 3146 5900
www.tivolihotels.com

Hotel Unique 029
Room rates:
double, US$655
Avenida Luís Antônio 4700
T 3055 4710
www.hotelunique.com.br

Uxua Casa Hotel 100
Room rates:
double, from US$800;
Casa da Árvore, US$1,140
Quadrado
Trancoso
T 73 3668 2277
www.uxua.com

WALLPAPER* CITY GUIDES

Executive Editor
Rachael Moloney

Editor
Jeremy Case

Authors
Paul McCann
Scott Mitchem

Art Director
Loran Stosskopf

Art Editor
Eriko Shimazaki
Designer
Lara Collins
Map Illustrator
Russell Bell

Photography Editor
Sophie Corben
**Contributing
Photography Editor**
Aisha Zia

Senior Sub-Editor
Nick Mee
Sub-Editors
Melanie Parr
Matt Sinha

Editorial Assistant
Emma Harrison
Interns
Geraldine Haneine
Candace Rardon

**Wallpaper* Group
Editor-in-Chief**
Tony Chambers
Publishing Director
Gord Ray
Managing Editor
Jessica Diamond

Contributors
Jeff Ares
Seth Kugel
Emma Moore
Tsuyoshi Murakami

Wallpaper* ® is a
registered trademark
of IPC Media Limited

First published 2007
Second edition (revised
and updated) 2011
© 2007, 2011 IPC Media
Limited

ISBN 978 07148 6273 6

PHAIDON

Phaidon Press Limited
Regent's Wharf
All Saints Street
London N1 9PA

Phaidon Press Inc
180 Varick Street
New York, NY 10014

Phaidon® is a registered
trademark of Phaidon
Press Limited

www.phaidon.com

A CIP Catalogue record for
this book is available from
the British Library.

All prices are correct at
the time of going to press,
but are subject to change.

Printed in China

PHOTOGRAPHERS

Leonardo Finotti
Memorial América Latina,
pp010-011
Pinacoteca do Estado,
p014, p015
Tivoli Mofarrej, pp022-023
Dalva e Dito, p036
D-Edge, pp038-039
Kosushi, p041
Forneria Villa Daslu,
pp042-043
Nbox, p048, p049
DOM, p050
Clos de Tapas, p051
Sonique Bar, pp052-053
Número, p054, p055
Bar Volt, pp056-057
Lorena 1989, p059
Melanie Bitti, p063
Museu Brasileiro de
Escultura, p065
Faculdade de Arquitetura
e Urbanismo, pp070-071
Rui Barbosa
Courthouse, p073
Auditório Ibirapuera,
pp074-075
Galeria Melissa, p081
Micasa Volume B,
pp082-083
Livraria da Vila, p085
Adriana Barra, pp086-087
Spa Cidade Jardim,
pp090-091
Sabina Escola, pp102-103

Michael Frantzis
Casa de Vidro, pp078-079

David Hughes
Ópera de Arame,
pp098-099

Nelson Kon
Fasano, p017
Museu de Arte de São
Paulo, pp066-067
Edifício Louveira,
pp076-077
SESC Fábrica
da Pompéia, p089
CEU Pimentas, pp092-093

**Stuart Franklin/
Magnum**
São Paulo city view,
inside front cover

Cristiano Mascaro
Rui Barbosa Courthouse
atrium, p072

Martin Müller
Edifício Bretagne,
pp068-069

Tuca Reinés
Edifício Copan, pp012-013
Fasano, pp018-019
Grand Hyatt, p020
L'Hotel, p024
Maksoud Plaza, p025

Hotel Unique, p029
Mercado Municipal, p033
Instituto Tomie
Ohtake, p037
Baretto, p044
Spot, pp046-047
Rodeio, p058
Restaurante Fasano,
pp060-061
Forum, p084
Jockey Club, pp094-095

**Reinhard Kliem/
Shapowalow**
Museu Oscar
Niemeyer, p097

SÃO PAULO
A COLOUR-CODED GUIDE TO THE HOT 'HOODS

JARDINS
Designer fashion stores and pricey real estate attract Brazil's legendary beauties

CENTRO
The southern hemisphere's answer to New York is bustling, edgy and on the way up

VILA MADALENA
This boho quarter is home to art galleries, eateries, bars and independent boutiques

ITAIM BIBI
Visit the commercial district after hours to discover São Paulo's most happening nightlife

HIGIENÓPOLIS
Clean-lined modernist blocks abound in this fascinating and laidback neighbourhood

PINHEIROS CENTRO
There's a huge variety of dining and socialising options in this thriving multicultural area

For a full description of each neighbourhood, see the Introduction.
Featured venues are colour-coded, according to the district in which they are located.